Leaving Xaia

Also by D. Nurkse

Staggered Lights
Isolation in Action
Shadow Wars
Voices Over Water

Leaving Xaia

D. Nurkse

FOUR WAY BOOKS

Marshfield

Editorial Office
Four Way Books
P.O. Box 607
Marshfield, MA 02050
www.gypsyfish.com/fourway

Library of Congress
Catalog Card Number: 98-75586

ISBN 1-884800-26-2

Cover Painting by Lucille Colin,
by permission of the artist.

Book Design: Henry Israeli

This book is manufactured in the United States of America and
printed on acid-free paper.

Four Way Books is a division of Friends of Writers, Inc.
a Vermont-based not-for-profit organization.
We are grateful for the assistance we receive from individual
donors and private foundations.

ACKNOWLEDGMENTS

Grateful acknowledgment is extended to the editors of the following magazines, for permission to reprint poems:

The Antioch Review: "The Background Chords Return in Minor"

Crosscurrents Quarterly: "Cordillera de los Espejos" [originally titled "Without Rain"]

Fine Madness: "Bring the War Home"

Five Fingers Review: "Flight Lounge"

Grand Street: "Ark River," "A Drive in the Coastal Range"

Hanging Loose: "The Twenty-Four Hour War," "The Checkpoints," "Absence Seizures," and "The Car Bomb"

The Hudson Review: "Peace After Long Sickness"

The Kenyon Review: "The Swiftness with Which Those Cities Fell," "Rooms by the Night or Hour"

Loblolly: "The River of Separation"

The Manhattan Review: "Marriage in the Largest City," "A Prayer of Abandonment," "The Assassination"

The Marlboro Review: "The Projects," "Letter from the Capital"

Nerve: "The Unlit Room"

The New Yorker: "A Night in Toluna"

Pivot: "The Soul"

Poetry: "Final Separation" [copyright © The Modern Poetry Association]

Poetry Northwest: "The Last Husband," "At Fulton Mall," "These Are Your Rights," and "Interior Highway"

Prism International: "The Final Chance," "The Road to Soria" [printed under the title "The Road to Ko"], "The Impending Famine at Xaia"

The Quarterly: "The Brackish Wells" and "The Guards"

The Washington Review: "Looking and Finding"

West Branch: "A Pause at Delta Assembly," "These Are Your Rights," "Customs," "The Interior," "The United States Embassy in Salvador," "Lateness," "Leaving Xaia" [printed under the title "Leaving Colombia"], "The Coming Crash," "Overseas Accounts" and "Prayer at Mount Sinai Hospital"

Thanks to the editors of Four Way Books, for permission to reprint "Leaving Xaia" [published under the title "Leaving Colombia"] and "Customs" from *The Four Way Reader #1*.

"Final Separation" was included in *Poetry Breaks*, a series of videocassettes produced by WGBH-Boston, and distributed by the Public Broadcasting Service.

"Cordillera De Los Espejos" appeared under the title "Without Rain" in *Anthology of Magazine Verse/Yearbook of American Poetry*, Monitor Books, California, 1988.

Thanks to the Mrs. Giles Whiting Foundation and the National Endowment for the Arts, for generous grants which allowed this book to be completed, and to the MacDowell Colony, Yaddo, Virginia Center for the Creative Arts, and Blue Mountain Center.

This book is dedicated to Ragnar Nurkse.

Special thanks to Martha Rhodes.

CONTENTS

Part One: Marriage in the Largest City

Part Two: A Block North of Mercy

Part Three: The Checkpoints

I

MARRIAGE IN THE LARGEST CITY

THE CAR BOMB

There was a murder at the corner
and the police left the body
cordoned off, waiting
for superior experts:
detectives, chemists, those who draw
chalk lines. Through the night
as the mood took us, we drifted back
taking our place in the crowd of spectators
that changed constantly because of the cold.
And the rumors changed, from drugs
to numbers to race. But each witness
wondered at the precision,
almost dispassionate, of that hate:
the body sitting at attention,
untouched face, chest blown open,
becoming familiar as the hours passed
towards dawn, so that sleepless children
ran up to the window, calling
obscene names, until the police flashlight
wheeled and focused on their eyes,
dazzling them, driving them back
to the narrow houses of our street.

THESE ARE YOUR RIGHTS

The counterdemonstrators were waiting
at the bottom of the street
and their poverty shocked us.
Bricks in paper bags,
bats, hoarse voices shouting
faggots, these streets are ours.
The space between our ranks
and theirs seemed living,
a strip of noon where dust
and blowing wrappers
were imbued with will.
They stared there too,
not meeting our eyes,
as if reading a signal
in that narrowing gap.
We began to sing,
they found a chant,
we struggled to hear their words
under our harmony,
the distance between us
no bigger than a body.
They spat and some of us
who sang swallowed that spit.
They parted, we kept marching,
they were an audience,
as they faded behind us
we could piece together words:
faggots, these streets are ours.
Then we turned into the green suburb,
the boulevard of carved maples,
dwarves with chipped lamps
painted white, and there
the line of squad cars

parked slantwise was waiting,
the visor raised a bullhorn
into its shadow and the voice
—pure metal—articulated:
These Are Your Rights.

OVERSEAS ACCOUNTS

Nights I worked beside you
in Automotive Empire

shipping fans and mufflers
to Cyprus, Ceylon,

Accra, the Windward Islands:
always you coughed,

the jute dust had entered your lungs.
Because I was in love with you

I imagined you were pretending,
coaxing me to touch you:

in my mind I stroked your back
until you were calm, breath came easy,

but my hands never lost their count,
as if it would always be the past,

arranging stamps, twine, bills of lading
according to a code of weight and distance

entered in a book too heavy to close.

BRING THE WAR HOME

We marched in lockstep
and later at the rally

we held hands briefly
and I had to keep coming back

to the Mark Clark vigil
and the fast in the cemetery

scared stiff of the police
—invisible cameras, visible sticks—

but hoping to see you
one more time or at least

hear the tremor of your voice
among those voices, massed like clouds.

ROOMS BY THE NIGHT OR HOUR

Remember how we used to meet
in a neighborhood of butcher shops,
zinc windows, storefronts
blank as canal water
with traces of gold lettering?

Remember the clerk's thumb
finding an empty page
in the greasy ledger?

I followed you upstairs.
Scared to look,
I shook when I unzipped you.

The tap leaked
as we lay in silence
and each drip was our future—
engagement, marriage, divorce.

Sometimes strange lights
flew across the ceiling—
a jet passing, a chopper,
the souls of the dead
jealous of our want.

We were so in love
we held hands when we came.

It was then I discovered
I didn't know you.
Your matted hair
covered my eyes.

Always we left at dawn
on tiptoe, terrified
of waking the legal couples,
while the clerk snored,
hidden by last night's news.

A PAUSE AT DELTA ASSEMBLY

When the foreman brought my pay
it was sixty dollars short.
I complained, my voice cracked,
he smiled and said,
you must have been sick.
The shop steward advised me,
file a grievance in ninety days.
I told the man beside me
on the line: he put my check
in his pocket, signalled,
          the line stopped,
the crankcases stopped, suddenly
just things, no longer
hours cased in steel:
there was a deep silence,
a force like loneliness,
you could hear the flies, high up,
rubbing against the kleig lights:
then the owner came to me
and opened his wallet, saying
I found your missing days.

MIDNIGHT AT THE COBALT HOTEL

You look tired
and a little skeptical
in your faded green dress,

and yet you're about to teach me
happiness, that deep art
without which body
and soul are nothing:

somewhere downtown
a great clock booms
and you lift your head,
counting under your breath:

then you tap your foot
to a music so faint
I never heard it in life.

DOMINANT HARMONY

The musicians practiced all night,
all day, all the next night.
Sometimes we hammered on the pipes
but they played in time,
however random our blows
they found a pattern to obey.
They repeated the same phrase
until it became infantile,
then pure genius, then silence,
then a flaw hidden in silence.
When we knocked and walked in
they didn't look up; when we asked
what are you preparing for?
they answered benevolently
though we could sense they were counting
in complex meter even as they spoke,
fingering their instruments, never losing
their place in the score,
but obliged to respond
because we were lovers, subjects
of the songs they'd memorized in every key.

LOOKING AND FINDING

Each dawn I left you
in my pressed shirt, carfare in my shoe,
and in some suburb of the infinite city
I pretended I could lay tile,
tap morse or play trombone.
Always I was sent home
by early afternoon, almost
          relieved to have failed,
and we weighted the drapes with books
and naked on top of each other
we pretended to be rain,
city roofs, the pistons
of the factory, the surge
of distant cars, even
the mirror's dazzling emptiness.

INTERIOR HIGHWAY

I was happy with you
and didn't know it
on the road to Centerville.

There should have been a billboard
saying PARADISE, each letter underscored
with a tiny lampblack shadow.

Instead of those dark outlets
selling fringed moccasins,
each with a string of lightbulbs
painted in peeling pastels.

Or that plywood bear cut-out
you would have stopped to photograph
except you left your camera in Malone.

There should have been signs
warning, we didn't know ourselves,
and giving the distance to each other
in miles and kilometers,
bad jokes and brief elegant silences.

Perhaps also a map
indicating the highest possible happiness
and marking scenic viewpoints,
guide booths and picnic tables.

Love, there were just fields
and occasionally a lit window
exercising its power over darkness.

Just the feeling of entering
a stranger's life
and leaving everything behind
without regret or even knowledge.

This is the one turn I hadn't imagined—
that peace would lie in going
and never returning,
that the gauge lights would flash at random
and I'd listen only to your tone of voice
as you told the plot of a movie
so complicated even you were lost.

Because I felt nothing
I wrote the word HAPPINESS
in red ink on the palm of my hand
between the life line and love line,

and it had faded to a blur
by the time we arrived at the exit,
at the motel, at happiness.

A DRIVE IN THE COASTAL RANGE

She put her coat over her head
and said: talk about me
as if I weren't here.

I said, she fascinated me.
She was like my life,
close and yet hidden.

We had come to the high orchards.
A pyramid of windfall apples
flashed and receded.

I wished she'd seen it.
I was scared of sex
and growing old.

She said: talk about me,
not some world
you'll never see again.

ARK RIVER

You pinned your hair
before entering the mud.

Afterwards you told me
how the reeds pulled at you
stubbornly but with no will,
how scared you were
of fighting that cling,
drawn into the old struggle
against no enemy.

I saw nothing: on the float
your face was like a child's,
laughing and counting breath.

We walked back barefoot
and the pebble road
made us dancers
to faint staccato music.

In the cabin, a green fly
zoomed against the bulb,
then retreated
to distant corners.

We dried each other
with cupped hands
until our nakedness
was like the crest of the wave
when you can almost see through it.

You let down your hair
and flicked the switch.
I heard your laughter
and the whine of the fly,
perhaps like us, far from home.

MARRIAGE IN THE LARGEST CITY

1

We were searched, entering
that enormous courthouse.
You were taken aside by a woman
in rubber gloves, I by a man.
They passed us through the metal detector
and patted our bodies scrupulously.
They made small talk across the curtain,
perhaps a couple themselves;
middle-aged, discussing pension plans,
their keychains jangling softly.
And we smiled confidently.
What could they find
that was not common knowledge?

2

We walked back from the registrar's office
in the drizzle of high air conditioners,
footsteps distinct—wife, husband—
shadows fusing on streaked walls.

We turned the key and entered
the room where we once lived together.

A few dishes in the sink,
a novel open to a marked page,
two empty glasses touching,
a calendar with all the days crossed out.

3

A fly landed on my belly
and flew to yours.
We knew we'd have the child,
drain each other, grow old.
We set the bargain then:
we'd show no mercy.
It was dusk. On Gates Avenue
voices swelled in praise of smoke.
The striated shadow of the blind
made our bodies a flight of steps.
Sirens grew faint. A cloud of flies
thudded softly outside the screen.

THE PROJECTS

At the corner of Madison and Jefferson
two plainclothes in a Plymouth Fury
picked up a drunk by his muscle tee-shirt
and cuffed him high behind his back.
A woman drifted down from the stoops
with a baby in her arms and blew a kiss.
The man turned and spat.
            I had been married
five years and my wife and child were sleeping
on Court Street. Instinctively I looked back
across the walls covered with ads for painkillers,
the dusty elms, the homeowners' naked trellises,
            when I turned the woman had disappeared
into the blur of radio voices and the prisoner
was rocking back and forth in silence.
The detectives had turned the engine off.
One stared straight at me without meeting my eye,
the other licked his fingers and began writing
slowly in an immense calfbound book,
and I kept walking, diminishing in that gaze,
past identical stoops, stepwise windows,
the yards with plaster dwarves in chipped boots,
the howls of dogs whose faces I will never see,
the madonnas, the old women who appear at gates
with their hands out, sensing a rain too fine to feel.

A CONFIDENTIAL BULLETIN

1

A neighbor calls at noon:
he has access to private security:
the riot engulfed our child's school.
I drift out. The day is bright and calm.
Chestnuts flare by the park entrance.
The laundromat is full of customers.
Some passersby are like me,
walking sideways, looking for help
from the profiles in passing cars.

2

At the dismissal gate
it turns out to have been a dream.
There was no overturned car, no looting,
no snipers chanting "next time."
Just a handful of parents, flustered,
arriving a few minutes early,
exchanging stories:

when we were children
the riots were more affectionate,
if you lived in the community
you were acknowledged and spared,
the lines were carefully drawn
down Cypress Avenue and Livonia.
Now there is this terrible randomness,
bullets that fly at whim,
fires that never happened,
and if there is a method
it will only be apparent later
as in a conversation
where everyone remembers what not to say.

THE ASSASSINATION

We pick our way
through scalloped glass.
A TV on the curb
reflects our pallor.
A vacuum cleaner
trails its cord.

We are tired, you and I.
We will have to have a long talk.
As always, we'll never see each other again
unless desire can lure us
deeper into our argument.

Madison, Jefferson, Hamilton.
We haven't seen a soul.

At Adams, a drunk on a stoop
puts down his pint of muscatel
and mumbles into a walkie talkie.

On Lincoln, the softball game
has re-convened.
A boy in a Giants tee shirt
stands whiffing Spaldeens
in mock amazement.

Our block is untouched.
We climb the dim steps
enter the single room
and sit facing each other

until the sirens return,
a magnesium flare bathes us
in icy light, at last
the narrow bed shudders
with the whine of helicopters.

AT FULTON MALL

A woman tried to leave
without paying, and Security
is trying to determine
the value of her meal.
Did she have the Surfburger?
With fries? With fried onions?
Tomato is extra.
Tartar sauce comes with it.
He asks the Deputy beside her
who relays the questions.
They're both old men
in colorcoded blazers
but Security has a palm tree
airbrushed on his tie.
He leans over the menu
and clicks a calculator.
He might be adding
the years I spent with you.
The Deputy makes small talk
through the many silences.
How about those Rams?
Dolphins? Vikings? Raiders?
The woman glances behind her
toward the street where a clock
must show how late she is.
To me, she looks like you
but gray with fatigue,
a house dress, a purse
that knocks against her knees.
The door is bright with snow
and a crowd passes there,
entering and leaving, each

giving her one quick glance.
When they see the handcuffs
they know as much as I.
At the far end of the counter
the waitress coaxes catsup
from an empty bottle to a full,
wincing at the time it takes.
Once I leave I notice:
my hand in my pocket
counting change mechanically.
I realize there was a radio
playing all that time
and a soft voice singing

each night I cry my eyes out
remembering the love we shared.

LIBERTY

I could not imagine knowing you
without knowing you always. I've
come to a place to stop.

Quiet as a Catskills city
with the bridge washed out
and Greyhound on strike.

Empty as a furnished room
with a peg on the door,
a view of dark hotels.

A note in the Bible
promises, if I sleep here
I'll wake in The City.

FINAL SEPARATION

My lawyer put his fingers together
and began confiding a strategy
to defend my rights to my child.
As he spoke in a stage whisper,
accenting the names of hostile judges,
my mind went slack and my eyes wandered
to the expensive view:

the park, the wharves,
the cities of Jersey
whose names run together:
Hoboken. . . Secaucus . . . Weehawken. . .

In the afternoon haze, four light planes
were skywriting with exquisite precision
but the wind took their message
and unravelled it like a skein:
a politician angling for votes?
A lover trying to reach a lost one?

Then the attorney coughed
and offered his faintly scented hand.
The documents were drawn and sealed,
that crisp Holland bond
almost tense as living flesh,
a tiny gap marked with a cross
where my name was already written.

THE UNLIT ROOM

What I liked about loving you
was being no one,

looking out the window afterwards,
showing you the laundry, the flag,

little ruled streets
where someone once met you,

adored you, persuaded you
to climb the narrow steps

pausing at each landing, waiting
for the heart to stop racing.

II

A BLOCK NORTH OF MERCY

THE TWENTY-FOUR HOUR WAR

Before the first air strike
the protests were so huge
we could not find our way to the edge,
desperate to find someone to convince,
the witnesses more fervent than the marchers . . .
Now the bombing has lasted three weeks,
ground war is inevitable and we're alone
behind a card table on Fifth and Prospect
with a petition demanding the Geneva Convention
be respected and evacuation corridors
established for women and children.
No one signs and we would no longer know
where to send it and the crowd
tightens around us:
            at last an old man
with gold teeth puffs his chest
in our faces and shouts:
            these are the terrorists . . .
            they love Saddam . . .
            they support the poison gas attacks . . .
The crowd relaxes, eyes flicker down
and we feel reprieved:
so long as he keeps screaming,
no harm will come to us.

THE SWIFTNESS WITH WHICH THOSE CITIES FELL

1. No Talks

That August, reflections grew very bright
and flickered at the edges
and appeared on land as well as water.

Two faces from the screen
glided through the crowd,
one a father, strict but fair,
the other in shadow.

There were voices offstage
to praise the fire
hidden in reason, the laser,

the wind in the nucleus: other voices,
equally calm, explained the desert,

how waiting here will break a man.

2. A Skirmish at El-Nejd

War to extinction
against a country we've never seen.

The recon flights last forever.
A pilot returns, telling the camera:
"I saw a fire creep up to me.
But I was out of reach."

Reports from hidden witnesses
of polio, cholera,
diseases from other centuries.

The wells changing hands,
then the mirages,
then the smoke.
The line of retreat on fire.

Was it two minds or one
that waited for this
quivering, chose it, conjured it

out of vague documents
and the dazzling heat of El-Nejd?

3. The Air Bridge

We bombed
until the enemy was immortal,
we bombed until he was dust,
we bombed a few more weeks:

our satellites disclosed his trenches
glowing with phosphorous:

was there a mind there
still living, or just a device

tripwired to return our fire?

4. The Absolute Ruler

If we could rid the world
of that one face

if we could cut it
from the paper
leaving a hole
singed at the edges

if we could block it
from the screen
with a crown of static

if we could turn those eyes
away from us

his secret police could remain in Basra
and his gunships patrol the North.

5. The Human Shield

Why did he put mothers and children
in the air-raid shelter
where we could kill them?

Why did he leave conscript soldiers
to face us, on pain of death,
without armor or water?

Who was he?
A shadow that had crossed a line
between childhood and death?

A voice speaking triumphantly
in an indecipherable code,
promising God's paradise
to those who could hold out against us
until the furnace of summer
and the coming of the great winds.

6. The Will to Resist Must Fade

My great-grandfather combs
in the dim mirror.

The swiftness with which those cities fell
reminds him of something
—he can't remember what it is.
He straightens his cravat.

What he wants we all want.
Unconditional surrender. It is at hand.

7. The Windy Season Offensive

After the parachutists disguised as leaves
and the alleged mugging behind the mirror
and looking down in winter from a glass cliff
and deciding to be happy,
          everywhere I go
I meet the survivors:
in subways, in museums,
one of them will come at me without swerving
as if to ask for a light, or a cigarette, or news,
and then turn, like a sack of air emptying:

I want to know what you expect from me,
faces that survive me.

8. A Prayer for News

In the middle of a meal
we checked the dial:

without the voice
we had no hunger:

in the act of love
we watched:

sometimes just traffic,
or sports, or weather,

or weather in Baghdad
—sometimes the dreams of experts.

What were we staring at?
Why did we imagine it was the war?

LETTER FROM THE CAPITAL

Je vous écris d'un pays lointain . . .
—Henri Michaux—

She writes: are there homeless in your city?
Do they come up to you
and show you a wound
and ask, *do you doubt my suffering?*

And do you pay?
Do you choose a quarter,
two dimes, or a nickel?
Is it the value of misery
you are trying to determine
as you grope in your pocket
while the stranger waits
with the calm face of a judge?

Are there trains full of people sleeping?
Surrounded by enemies, do they cover their eyes
with rags or newspaper,
afraid of the light, of sleeplessness?

And you yourself—
if you threw away the envelope
with my return address,
wouldn't you be lost too?

There is one old man
who always excuses himself,
saying, *I'm not your burden,*
but if I don't ask,
how will you know I'm hungry?

★

She continues:

Is the air sometimes so thick
when a person leaves your side
he becomes indistinct
after a few steps?

Is it an effort to speak
above the constant murmur?

If you fall silent a moment,
does someone else complete your thought?

*

I know drunks who make a point
of asking only for food
as a gauge of sincerity.
But who would trust a stranger's offering?
I never see them eat.

Some victims cannot change their stories:
each day, their house burnt yesterday.
Is it untrue, even if time passes?
If they were cheating,
couldn't they choose another grief?

The city has put up signs:
if you want to help,
give to a known charity.

*

Once I heard a barbershop quartet
swaying in four-part harmony,
smiling to keep their pitch up,
counting to maintain a trance,
practicing little gestures
of rapture or despair.

A cripple watched
and applauded in delight.

*

I gave the old man
my gold-tipped pen
and the picture I have of you
and he accepted politely,
as if they had value:
I gave him the letter
I'd written you, pledging love,
promising marriage and children,
and he thanked me gravely,
as if this was what he always wanted,
and nodded, and limped on
to the next stranger.

THE LAST HUSBAND

I met him at one of those receptions
I haunted after my divorce,
in a district of ballbearing factories,
stockyards, binderies and distilleries:

a man remarkably like me,
perhaps even more exhausted,
nibbling intently on a jumbo shrimp
as if watching a great secret
disappear before his eyes.

Was I eager to be exposed?
My tie was creased and threadbare.
I knew nothing of semi-pro hockey
or put-shares in the bauxite industry.

I had to drink almost as much
to talk to him as once to you,
but the chill wine was astonishing

and I found myself dreaming of home,
of the white bed and shivering curtain,
the breeze and the mysteries of sacred love:

as I drained my glass
he emptied his, and side by side
we gobbled the Calamata olives,
sushi, scones, melon cubes impaled
on toothpicks wrapped in green cellophane,
squid, rhubarb, endives, strawberries:

we spoke softly, like children in a trance,
of the starting line-up of the Harrisburg Huskies,
the vast deserted mines in Zambia
and the movements of money via satellite,

until the bay window darkened
and we saw our ghostly bodies
exchanging statistics, blessing each other,
unwilling to part or pronounce your name.

THE COMING CRASH

I'd become a stranger
and stood at the edge of conversations
with a filmy glass in my hand
—always the talk was of collapse,
steel gates over bank doors,
a riot spreading from city to city
the way pain travels the nerve paths.
I wanted to interject:

this breakdown was being forecast
when I was still a child,
before I married and divorced,
when my voice was used to being heard
and my hands to being touched
and my eyes to being seen:

but I'd become an echo,
an old man complaining
about a sweet his mother
denied him in the crib.

ABSENCE SEIZURES

Everyone knew the man who wheeled me
and had a kind word for him,
for his wife and child
and his father in Barbados,
they even had a smile for me
or a quick wish for good luck
as we negotiated those corridors
under Mount Sinai,
past meat lockers, loading docks,
a vault of chipped crucifixes,
a bank of computers, dumpsters,
            then the lead-sealed door
and the halls color-coded
for the parts of the body:
kidney, liver, heart, mind.

THE SOUL

You can stand aside
and watch what pain does to you
as if it happened to a stranger.
The surgeons may crowd you aside,
mistaking you for the orderly
who waits with a tray of knives.
But you will not be the one lying
where the magnesium lights converge.
You will be a bystander,
free to drift into the lobby
and flip through a magazine,
to leave and tell the guard
you lost your entry pass.

If you are held at all, what holds you
is only words: *the sorrow of the flesh.*

A PRAYER AT MOUNT SINAI HOSPITAL

I am teaching myself
to imagine an acorn
without thinking "oak"
and to consider a lit window
without thinking "home."

How to learn these skills?
I have surrounded myself
with the great treatises—
massive volumes, goldflecked,
the calfskin bindings
buckling, the print so fine
I must eke it out
inch by inch with a glass.

Each night the orderly
mops the long corridor
and sings the songs of Zion
—how to listen
and not think "freedom"?

I bite my tongue
when I tell myself:

you too will pass
through the needle's eye,
stretching your arms out
comfortably in all directions,
sensing only darkness
and the hum of the life support.

THE POWER DOOR

My doctor says:
What do you remember
of your former life?

Everything, I answer.
My wife's face
when she still loved me.
The child in the stroller
wailing for milk.
The cars endlessly passing.
Two voices behind the wall,
one happy, one sad—

The doctor holds up his hand.
Enough. That was the easy test.
Now I must walk on my heels
from the bed to the curtain
and return on tiptoe.
I must touch my nose,
count backward from a hundred,
and begin signing the huge forms
too thick to staple.

Once more I must pass
through the electric eye
and walk among the crowds
with my own cloud of breath,
my token in my pocket,
an inscribed bracelet
and a xerox'd map,
the cross-streets smudged
and the way home drawn
in red ink by a heavy hand.

PEACE AFTER LONG SICKNESS

At first you would visit me
only a few minutes at a time.
The door opened and you entered
—you and pain, like two guests
who know each other by accident.
Then you began to stay.
Sometimes you glanced at your wrist
subtly, disguising the gesture
in a series of chores and fidgets,
and I felt a pang of jealousy.
Soon you were passing the night
in the metal chair, dozing all day
like me, plying the edges of a trance.
When I woke, you opened the curtain
that you closed while I slept.
I could no longer imagine this room
without your slightly sagging shoulders.
I explained the mysteries of my fever
to you, how it was like riding a train,
feeling motionless and then watching
tall houses recede, but instead of walls
flying past me, there were years,
days, seconds. You nodded and in turn
told me the story how we became lovers:
rain, the suntan lotion leaking
in a soaked picnic hamper,
a barn, the straw absurdly hard
like an armchair with broken springs
—afterwards, we found lumps of coal
imbedded in it—and as you spoke
it was as if it had been true always,
I felt my life taking root

in the breath that shaped your words.
When I asked for news of our city
you paused, genuinely trying to remember,
running your fingers through my hair.
I knew it was the winter of the riots,
but it was as if I'd read the words
in a phrasebook in a foreign language.
You sang to me. You were so close
if I shut my eyes you were no closer,
and the pain was very remote,
a silhouette in a dazzling window
deeper in the maze of hospitals.

A BLOCK NORTH OF MERCY

I miss the moans
of the incurable ward,
the clinking bedpans,
the radio's consolation.

A younger patient
needed my narrow bed,
tight plastic bracelet
and glass of cloudy water.

Who am I now
without that chart
that dipped and jumped
at the will of fever?

All praise to the mask
who healed me with a knife.
Now I pray for patience
until the light changes.

III

THE CHECKPOINTS

THE IMPENDING FAMINE IN XAIA

In the great hall an official
is demonstrating the projected shortfall.

He has unfurled a graph
and a map of the coastal plain.

He holds up a picture
of a marketplace at noon.
In a year none of these people will be living.

But from the audience, you can hardly distinguish
the huddled bodies from the pyramids of fruit.

Perhaps the photo was taken long ago.

*

And there are others waiting to testify.

One has a metal briefcase
and drums on it with his fingers
until angry glances shush him.
Another cradles a laptop
and is lost in the tiny columns
as if staring into a fire.
One keeps documents
wadded in all his pockets,
sheaves of figures
folded into tiny clumps,
and as he waits he pats himself.
Another carries a mailing tube
—perhaps charts?—another

rests a projector on his knees.
They sit on folding chairs
on the podium and flanking the steps
into the press lounge
and out the fire door.

And the audience?

The delegates are reading the paper,
trying to find out the weather
in their own countries,
or baseball scores,
or the faces of their rulers.

One drinks from a flask.
Another takes notes
—a cloud of tiny zeroes—
his face gray with fatigue.

⋆

She says: "Some nights all I want
is to see the world without me—
to disappear without hurting anyone."
The walls here are paper thin.
All night, keys clink in other locks.
Faint laughter, and we yearn
to hear the punchline.
I answer her with a kiss;
she seems comforted.
Before dawn, all we hear
is the ice machine rattling
and the hum of monitors.

⋆

Late for the hearings,
we pass the first hunger strikers.
A man and a woman in the costume
of the villages of the interior.
He wears a black bowler,
a suit with white piping
and rusted epaulettes.
She is cinched in a hooped skirt.
He hugs a hand-lettered sign
explaining the demands.
A clipboard holds a blank petition
with a pen tied to a string.
Propped at their feet is a calendar
where the days will be marked off
beginning with this one.

⋆

Was it her voice I heard and could no longer comfort,
raised above the murmur in the corridor,
singing the bitterness of kwashiorkor?
It was a single marcher
—then an army of voices,
shouting No and a counter-voice
shouting either a word or a name:
not Xaia or a hill village:
repeated, it frayed at the edges,
a heart beating faster and faster.

But when I peeked out the washroom window
I saw only a handful of peasant women
huddled in shawls or felt blankets
surrounded by riot police.

All their faces were slack with sleeplessness
even at that distance.

⋆

In the great hall, a microphone explains:
A hundred ships loaded hull-down with wheat
are moored on sea-anchor outside Ko.
But the draught is too shallow.

★

Sometimes an usher taps my shoulder.
I thread my way out of the conference room.
Her voice on the red phone says she's changed her life.
Or she leaves a message on my machine:
she's saved, she's leaving.

She'll be a potter or a weaver.
She'll grow melons,
one for herself, one for her neighbor,
in a hot country where land is cheap.

She no longer believes that love is hunting her
through the mirror-maze of cities.

It is only a voice that proclaims this
endlessly, in her sleep, and like the other echoes
it will fall silent and she'll hear

a mother chanting to her child,
the maize pulverized under the pestle,
the bees returning to the shattered hive.

THE RIVER OF SEPARATION

A friend went to the famine zone.
When he came back his eyes
would not meet mine.
Once he let me into his silence
and told of standing on a bridge
watching the bodies pass
bloated with hunger, faces
blank from the current.
When he finished I dreamt
of that bridge every night
until I spoke of it
as if I'd been the one
standing there—especially
to a woman, and she believed,
and was marked, and asked
for news; long after
I was gone, she begged for news
from everyone who knew me.

THE GUARDS

They held my passport
next to the torch
and I felt my features
dissolve in a clear pool
of black ink,
then the background
that had held me stiff
and beaming began to char:
the corporal waved it once
in a rain of sparks
and handed it to me
with a slight bow:
at once I stifled it
against my body,
scorching my last clean shirt:
I was allowed into Xaia.

THE FINAL CHANCE

Each night I wondered:
why don't they kill me?
There had been no wheat in that city
for three days . . . a week . . . .
The watersellers sat on their casks
drumming their ladles between their legs,
eyes huge with thirst: but each night
they were milder, more polite.
I walked at midnight through the crowds.
Men gambled, scooping up
their dice with great effort,
children stumbled after knotted rags,
arguing over boundaries.
Women sang softly
to babies too tired to sleep.
But no one looked at me.
No one spoke. If a tossed jack
bounced in my path
it was retrieved gingerly.
I thought bitterly:
can't they tell I'm here
by will, not accident?
Only the lottery-ticket seller
followed me until dawn,
rattling his dented tin cup,
chanting, Stranger, reciting
his inexhaustible list of numbers.

CORDILLERA DE LOS ESPEJOS

That summer of long drought
we tiptoed on the ridges
afraid of the friction
if we kicked two stones together:
as if the sierra were already flame
and we were locked in the past,
as if the world without rain
could only be real
in a flash: by night
in late August chill
we huddled at the campfire,
stamping on our sparks, cupping them
in our bare hands, staring out
at the coyotes' eyes
consumed with reflected fire.

THE ROAD TO SORIA

A funeral passed through the wheat,
a child's coffin surrounded
by guttering candles;
those who followed
sang, moaned and beat a drum.
          You asked me
Is it the hardness of life here
that makes them so sure of paradise?
          I couldn't answer.
No matter how they whirled,
the dancers' eyes remained averted.

THE BRACKISH WELLS

I was weakened by a long sickness
I thought was the coming of God.
I thought my life
was narrowing to a point
like fire when the wind drops,
like a road in a drawing:

but it was the work of fever,
a cloud in the water,
a breeze that tasted
of the insides of the body.

Do you remember visiting me,
your arms full of white lilies?
Or was that a fever dream?

I would have insisted
I was close to absolute mastery.

Night after night I was certain
I felt the Messiah's hand
touch my forehead, and his voice
murmur in my ear

many names, yours and mine,
then yours alone.

A PRAYER OF ABANDONMENT

Pain has been very patient with me,
teaching something of terrible importance.
Night after night I still don't understand—
is it a word or a gesture?
A name, a color or a face?

I am a slow student
at wit's end with myself.
If the test were tonight
all I could recite
would be: Clock, Mirror,
Curtain, Vase, Darkness.

I have not even mastered
the steps receding in the hall.

DAWN OR TWILIGHT

In my sickbed at Soria
I heard a voice in the street
saying, *walk, walk,*
raised clearly over the shouts
of pushers selling crack,
the ravings of drunks,
the sleepless peddlers crying:
apples, bread, milk.

THE INTERIOR

I don't want to go
too deep into Xaia again.
Not past the wells
into the black onyx desert.
Not so deep in love
I lie beside you as you sleep
feeling your breath on my cheek
like a door closing.
Not back to the plain of voices
where I spoke your name
and the cairns and stunted trees
called you, and the hawk
answered with its remote cry,
its almost slow plunge.
There must be a blaze
that shows where to stop.
So that if my mind and body
continue, I can still wait
in safety on the near side
of a line etched with a twig.
The guide says:

Region of great poverty.
Products: flax, jute.
Laborers willing to work
for rice and water.
Alum for mirrors.
Knives. Brooms. Maps
of the roadless interior.
Wine for the faceless God.

A NIGHT IN TOLUNA

Always that knocking
at the iron door,
and that voice whispering
what if I open?

Then silence.
A raindrop in the courtyard.
The gurgle of the pump.

A hen rustling
her dusty feathers
in a sleep I can't share.

Again the pounding,
terrified but also
as if there were no one—

just moonlight
and the granite road
climbing to the Andes.

Soon I'll hear the heavy bolt
being drawn back,
the moan of the hinge
and the dog barking incredulously.

It will be day, and never again
will I dream I saw your face.

CUSTOMS

Children came running,
naked or in frayed shorts,
bellies wobbling on bird's-legs.
I put my hand in my pocket
for change, but when they came near
they spat at me, eyes burning
with a contempt I'd never imagined.
They shouted, "when you come to Santa Ana
the police will put you in jail
forever," and they laughed,
they cursed me, they spat until tears
came to my eyes. I asked:
"how far is the frontier":
looking ahead I could see red dust,
row after row of streets,
palms rattling, zinc windows,
doors made from billboards
buckling inward. The children laughed
and screamed, "we'll take you there."
They knotted around me
matching my steps, once
a stone hummed past my ear,
then they were gone,
I was in the next country,
a guard passed back my papers
and I walked alone in the dust
in the street of old men, my fist
still frozen on its clump of pennies.

THE UNITED STATES EMBASSY IN SALVADOR

Under the fifty-foot wall
the machine gunners had us check
our keys, penknives, cameras,
lens cases, metal combs,
then we passed through the sensors,
the X-rays, the corridor of pictures
of Jesus and the Beatles, and we sat
in the auditorium while the attaché
explained how the killings
had receded, and unfurled
a graph big as a flag with a black line
plummeting from 10,000 to sixty-two.
He described how the Archbishop died
in infinite detail, then announced
"this world is violent" and the interview
was over, we left relieved
we'd allowed the rage to dance
in the statistics, not quiver
in our voice and deliver
us to him: in the courtyard
the sun sealed our eyes,
the guards counted out
crucifixes, ballpoints,
coins with edges worn sharp,
and we stepped out
into the lines of those who wait
permanently, the widows,
the amputees, the visa sellers,
who parted, as if by instinct,
without looking at us, perhaps
knowing us by scent, or the heaviness
of our footsteps, and let us pass.

THE BACKGROUND CHORDS RETURN IN MINOR

You move through this room
touching one person's sleeve,
another's cheek.
How easily you make us laugh,
coax us to forget the curfew,
make us talk about ourselves
as if we were free.
You know the great exhaustion
that comes from growing old
in a city of shifting alliances.
You understand how sleepless waiting
for something we cannot even name
—a child's voice, a scent on the breeze—
has made us stiff like statues
propped together. For you
there is no more consequence,
whoever has weapons is the government,
and the one you wake with
is the one you love.
Still you forgive our ravenous attack
on the watercress canapés,
our jitters at the faint sirens:
we're condemned to discuss the news
passionately, absentmindedly,
as if the bombings were pure chance:
you know we'll always need the tact
of your supernatural fatigue,
your transparent porcelain,
every modulation of your constant music.

FLIGHT LOUNGE

There were walls of people
desperate to leave Salvador.
We stood in line among stone-faced peasants,
farmers with chickens in canvas bags,
deserting soldiers in battle regalia . . .
we whispered to each other,
"if we are truly desperate
like them, it makes no sense
to wait" and we shoved them aside,
waving our passports, shouting
"America" until at last we came
to the island of calm,
the corridor protected by Lawrence Welk,
the computer and the clerk
with the beatific smile,
ushering us to the alcove
cordoned off by machine guns
where we could wait
just by standing still.

LEAVING XAIA

A hand came from behind
and took me by the throat,
a van door opened,
I was taken to a tiny house
down a path flanked with conch shells
a block from the barracks.
There I was stripped
and the hood put over me.
As I stood facing the wall
palms pressing concrete
I began to dream of you
so intently, as if my mind
had created you
and could sustain you,
as if your face
were all that could last,
almost my last obstacle:
then the voice commanded
dress, I dressed in silence,
I was ushered out,
I heard the whine of props,
my sight was returned,
so were my papers,
a soldier escorted me
up the boarding ramp.
I took my place
among the other tourists;
in the porthole the night roads
dipped and faded,
either to open sea
or to a city without light.

LATENESS

Walking at night in a foreign city
you come to the golden windows.
In one a pair of lovers embraces:
in another an old man sits
rocking, sucking his thumb:
the next discloses an empty room
with a table set for supper:
the last holds a mother
giving suck to a child.
Then you walk on
among the broad dusty streets,
rows of houses curiously unfinished,
missing roofs or doors, mounds
of earth even on the sidewalks,
sometimes a violin repeating
a scrap of obsessive argument,
but no light except for the high
abstract glare of stooping lamps:
and you realize you were home
there, in front of the windows,
those were the golden cards
dealt you: when you walk back,
that street—if it is the right street—
is dark like all the others,
but you hear the whimpering of the child.

THE CHECKPOINTS

At crossroads after crossroads
the military asked you for papers,
sometimes friendly, sometimes begging
for a cigarette, or a coin
in your currency, or baseball news,
sometimes shouting, calling you
whore, faggot, child, old man,
sometimes pointing the gun
straight into your mouth
and waiting, sometimes handing you
pictures of Jesus or revolutionary tracts,
daring you to take them, sometimes
asking you politely to wait
—then the day became a life
already lived, now surplus,
in that elastic time
you felt yourself become a helmet
reflected in a filthy window
while they called into radios
and music answered. Once
they took your papers
and you felt your soul dying
but they brought them back
with a neat stamp: war zone.
Behind their dusty epaulettes
you glimpsed a city
that never quite ended:
shacks full of rusty turbines,
boilers, bits of conveyor belts,
files of old men waiting to vote
or children waiting for milk:
then open country:

dusty plains, empty
except for waterbuffalo
and cinders drifting:
sun heavy as a tombstone:
you squinted at the ribbon
of red dust and learned
to slow for culverts, thorn hedges,
blind curves, and not to answer
if a peasant waved from the fields.
Suddenly you were in the mountains.
Range after range, burning
as if serenely, in the sky
ranges of twisting smoke.
The road ended. So you waited.
At dusk a whistle came.
An hour later, another.
Then a lamp wavered.
You called your name
as if you were already there,
in that dry river bed
under granite spurs glinting with heat,
and a silence answered, the first
since you came to that country:
only when dark fell could you hear
the faint crackle of distant fires,
a cricket, a guitar in the valley.
A voice said: come to us.
You obeyed and at once
the children had surrounded you:
they pointed scornfully
to their stumps, their bellies
bloated with hunger, and led you

to the banquet they had laid out:
pancakes in fat, corn
roasted in its husk,
clay pots of rice, and ordered you
in mime or in whispers:
eat.

D. Nurkse's previous books of poetry include *Shadow Wars, Isolation in Action, Staggered Lights,* and *Voices Over Water.* He has received two National Endowment for the Arts fellowships, the Whiting Writers' Award, and the 1998 Bess Hokin Prize from *Poetry*. In 1999, he received a New York State Foundation for the Arts Fellowship. He has also written widely on human rights. In 1996, he was appointed Poet Laureate of Brooklyn.

The Four Way Books Prize Selections in Poetry
1995-2001

AWARD SERIES:

Gravida Sue Standing, 1995, selected by Robert Pinsky

Funeral Pie Stuart Friebert, 1996, co-winner, selected by Heather McHugh

The Tension Zone Sarah Gorham, 1996, co-winner, selected by Heather McHugh

Radio Tooth Paul Jenkins, 1997, selected by Alberto Ríos

Smokes Susan Wheeler, 1998, selected by Robert Hass

INTRO SERIES:

Corporal Works Lynn Domina, 1995, selected by Stephen Dobyns

Be Properly Scared M. Wyrebek, 1996, selected by Gregory Orr

Eye of the Blackbird Mary Ann McFadden, 1997, selected by Chase Twichell

Strike Root Anne Babson Carter, 1998, selected by Grace Schulman

The Theory and Function of Mangoes George Kalamaras, 2000, selected by Michael Burkard

THE LEVIS POETRY PRIZE:

Absence, Luminescent Valerie Martínez, 1999, selected by Jean Valentine

4 Noelle Kocot, 2001, selected by Michael Ryan